GOVERNMENT ACCOUNTABILITY OFFICE REVIEW OF THE PRISONER OF WAR/ MISSING IN ACTION (POW/MIA) COMMUNITY AND THE RESTRUCTURING OF THESE AGENCIES AS PROPOSED BY THE DEPARTMENT OF DEFENSE

HEARING

BEFORE THE

SUBCOMMITTEE ON MILITARY PERSONNEL

OF THE

COMMITTEE ON ARMED SERVICES
HOUSE OF REPRESENTATIVES

ONE HUNDRED THIRTEENTH CONGRESS

SECOND SESSION

HEARING HELD
JULY 15, 2014

U.S. GOVERNMENT PRINTING OFFICE

89–510   WASHINGTON : 2015

For sale by the Superintendent of Documents, U.S. Government Printing Office,
http://bookstore.gpo.gov. For more information, contact the GPO Customer Contact Center,
U.S. Government Printing Office. Phone 202–512–1800, or 866–512–1800 (toll-free). E-mail, gpo@custhelp.com.

CONTENTS

CHRONOLOGICAL LIST OF HEARINGS

2014

Page

TUESDAY, JULY 15, 2014

GOVERNMENT ACCOUNTABILITY OFFICE REVIEW OF THE PRISONER OF WAR/MISSING IN ACTION (POW/MIA) COMMUNITY AND THE RESTRUCTURING OF THESE AGENCIES AS PROPOSED BY THE DEPARTMENT OF DEFENSE

STATEMENTS PRESENTED BY MEMBERS OF CONGRESS

WITNESSES

APPENDIX

GOVERNMENT ACCOUNTABILITY OFFICE REVIEW OF THE PRISONER OF WAR/MISSING IN ACTION (POW/MIA) COMMUNITY AND THE RESTRUCTURING OF THESE AGENCIES AS PROPOSED BY THE DEPARTMENT OF DEFENSE

———————

House of Representatives,
Committee on Armed Services,
Subcommittee on Military Personnel,
Washington, DC, Tuesday, July 15, 2014.

The subcommittee met, pursuant to call, at 2:00 p.m., in room 2212, Rayburn House Office Building, Hon. Joe Wilson (chairman of the subcommittee) presiding.

OPENING STATEMENT OF HON. JOE WILSON, A REPRESENTATIVE FROM SOUTH CAROLINA, CHAIRMAN, SUBCOMMITTEE ON MILITARY PERSONNEL

Mr. WILSON. Ladies and gentlemen, the hearing will come to order. I would like to welcome everyone to the Subcommittee on Military Personnel of the House Armed Services Committee, as we hear from witnesses on the planned reorganization of the POW/MIA [Prisoner of War/Missing in Action] accounting community of the Department of Defense.

Almost a year ago, this subcommittee held a hearing on GAO's [Government Accountability Office] report on their review of the Department's efforts to meet the 2010 mandate to identify 200 missing persons per year by 2015, and Dr. Paul Cole's report entitled "JPAC's [Joint POW/MIA Accounting Command] Information Value Chain, the Identification of Missing Persons."

The GAO report, and I hope our committee's interest in oversight on this issue, became what I believe is a catalyst for change. Reviews by the Office of the Cost Assessment and Program Evaluation and the Office of the Inspector General began shortly after the hearing; on 31 March 2014 Secretary Hagel announced the reorganization of the accounting community based on the recommendation of the reviews.

Today, the subcommittee will continue its oversight on this important issue to hear from our witnesses on how they came to the conclusions and recommendations announced by the Secretary and the way ahead for the reorganization for the POW/MIA accounting community.

The men and women both in uniform and DOD [Department of Defense] civilian personnel who perform this mission are very dedicated to this effort and have done incredible work in the past. I am confident they will continue as professionals as the Department moves forward with these efforts.

I am hopeful to move forward with this endeavor, as I firmly believe that we as a nation owe the proper emphasis, resources, and priority of effort to account for our missing persons from past conflicts and to bring closure to their family members.

I would like to welcome our distinguished witnesses. Dr. Jamie Morin, newly confirmed within the last month.

Dr. MORIN. Two weeks, sir.

Mr. WILSON. Two weeks—even better. So thank you and best wishes. Director of the Cost Assessment and Program Evaluation and DOD is so good on acronyms, CAPE.

Mr. Michael D. Lumpkin, Assistant Secretary of Defense, Special Operations/Low-Intensity Conflict, performing the duties of Under Secretary of Defense for Policy, Department of Defense.

Mrs. Davis, do you have any opening remarks?

[The prepared statement of Mr. Wilson can be found in the Appendix on page 21.]

STATEMENT OF HON. SUSAN A. DAVIS, A REPRESENTATIVE FROM CALIFORNIA, RANKING MEMBER, SUBCOMMITTEE ON MILITARY PERSONNEL

Mrs. DAVIS. Thank you, Mr. Chairman. I also want to extend a warm welcome to Secretary Lumpkin and to Dr. Morin. Thank you for being with us today.

Last year this subcommittee held a hearing that highlighted the dysfunction and the challenges that plagued the POW/MIA accounting community within the Department of Defense. As a result, Secretary Hagel took his responsibility head-on here and asked Assistant Secretary of Defense for Special Operations and Low-Intensity Conflict Lumpkin to lead this effort to resolve the many issues that confront this community.

The Secretary proposed to establish a single defense agency to consolidate and coordinate the vast activities that fall under the purview of the POW/MIA accounting community. The subcommittee supported this effort and included language in the fiscal year 2015 NDAA [National Defense Authorization Act] to create a more effective and efficient organization to be able to meet the goal of identifying at least 200 sets of remains a year by 2015.

While the consolidation and the establishment of a defense agency is a positive first step, it is important for us to understand what the final agency will be comprised of; how will the transformation and the consolidation of activities, personnel, and resources be accomplished, and what the timeline for these actions will be; and what is really a fair timetable for the Department to accomplish the proposal, and for the Congress and the American people, particularly the families and loved ones who have a service member who is missing or unaccounted for, to be able to hold the agency accountable for the increased transparency that the agency of course is saying that this will bring about, the transparency of the reporting and certainly the identifications as well.

Mr. Chairman, I know we have a moral responsibility to ensure that those who are missing and remain unaccounted for are returned home to their family and their loved ones. I happen to see an article just now where a granddaughter is searching for a grandfather who died back in 1952 and that's not unusual. We know that that occurs.

I look forward to hearing from our witnesses and having an open and a productive dialogue today as we move forward to fundamentally change the POW/MIA accounting community. Thank you, Mr. Chairman.

Mr. WILSON. Thank you, Ranking Member Susan Davis.

I now ask unanimous consent that Representative Richard Nugent and Tim Walz be allowed to ask questions during the hearing. Without objection, so ordered.

I also ask unanimous consent that Representative Glenn Thompson be allowed to submit a statement for the record. Without objection, so ordered.

[The information referred to can be found in the Appendix on page 47.]

Mr. WILSON. Dr. Morin, we will begin with your testimony. As a reminder, please keep your statements to 5 minutes. We have your written statements as well as Mr. Lumpkin's.

Additionally, very likely we will be interrupted with votes. We will recess and then come back. And then each member who would like would have the opportunity for a 5-minute question period. So thank you very much. Dr. Morin.

STATEMENT OF HON. JAMIE M. MORIN, DIRECTOR, COST ASSESSMENT AND PROGRAM EVALUATION, DEPARTMENT OF DEFENSE

Dr. MORIN. Mr. Chairman, Mrs. Davis, thank you very much for the invitation to testify today and for the committee's continued commitment to ensuring that our families of service members have the opportunity to get closure for those who remain missing from our Nation's conflicts.

The Department of Defense works very hard to ensure that we seek and recover the remains of our fallen heroes, and that we can bring that sort of closure to the families. We are able to do so thanks to the authorities and the appropriations that the Congress provides for that purpose. And so we very much appreciate the committee's continued support for that effort and engagement on the reform process in this area.

The Department very clearly has a solemn duty in this area to provide our families of the fallen with the fullest possible accounting. As you mentioned, in 2009, the Congress passed legislation requiring the Department to increase its personnel accounting capability, and set the goal of accounting for 200 missing personnel annually beginning in 2015.

Despite a very strong commitment from the leadership of the Department and the hard work of many dedicated men and women across the accounting community, when the Cost Assessment and Program Evaluation Office looked at the community's progress towards this metric, it was clear that fundamental reform was going to be required to put us on a path to achieve the legislative goal.

So in my testimony today, what I would like to do is update the committee on CAPE's recommendations for reforming an imperfect system. As this committee is very much aware, in July of last year, the GAO study laid out in a very strong report the fact that a fragmented organization structure undermined the Department's ability to accomplish this mission.

Deputy Secretary Carter tasked my office with responsibility to assess the efficiency and the effectiveness of the personnel accounting community's structure and their processes, and to evaluate whether the 200-accounted-for metric was a sufficient one for observing and evaluating the community.

If I can just summarize in capsule form, our study confirmed many of the findings of the GAO report and extended on them in some respects. We determined number one, that the Department should fundamentally reform the organizational structure of the personnel accounting community, and should do so by unifying the Defense Prisoner of War and Missing Personnel Office, which we call DPMO, and the Joint POW/MIA Accounting Command, which we call JPAC, into a single new civilian-led defense agency with a new name that brings together the missions.

Second, we recommended that the Department add a medical examiner as the lead authority for establishing formal identification within the personnel accounting process.

The third recommendation is that we rescope the activities of the Central Identification Laboratory and make that entity more focused and more efficient.

And then fourth, we recommend that the Department complement the annual accounted-for number goal with a broader range of appropriate metrics that really reflect the full range of efforts that are executed by the accounting community to include many activities caring for families of those lost. And our report includes a list of metrics for possible consideration.

So in addition to those main recommendations, CAPE also identified a number of process improvements within the personnel accounting organizations. First among these, to improve transparency by categorizing cases for all of our conflicts as either active pursuit cases or non-recoverable cases, and engaging with and informing family members of the case status and the reasons for categorization.

A second of these additional recommendations, and there are several more that I won't enumerate right now but are in the written report, is to establish a standard case management tool, really a database, that is accessible across the personnel accounting community, has accessibility for family members as well, and that includes all the appropriate restrictions and controls to protect data that needs to be protected, but also maximize transparency.

Our assessment is that these changes, along with many others that are identified in the report, will, if implemented, improve business practices and mission effectiveness throughout the community. And my team that worked on this report is closely collaborating with Mr. Lumpkin's team in the implementation effort.

Bottom line here, in the report last year, GAO stated top-level leadership attention is needed to address the personnel accounting issues. My assessment is that is exactly what is happening. The CAPE study team presented findings directly to Secretary Hagel. Secretary Hagel listened to those findings and that informed his decisions based on Mr. Lumpkin's recommendations to reorganize the community and improve its business processes.

Again, we are pressing forward on this effort. We very much appreciate the committee and the Congress' continued support. I wanted to just close by thanking the excellent CAPE staff, a few of whom are in the room right now, who worked on this effort, and I think produced actionable, concrete, real recommendations for the Secretary and Mr. Lumpkin that will help the Department to deliver on this important mission. Thank you.

[The prepared statement of Dr. Morin can be found in the Appendix on page 22.]

Mr. WILSON. Thank you very much. What a positive report. This is very unusual in Congress and—to see it coming together with common sense, so thank you very much.

And Mr. Lumpkin, we are having votes, and so 5 minutes, thank you and then we will recess and come right back.

STATEMENT OF HON. MICHAEL D. LUMPKIN, ASSISTANT SECRETARY OF DEFENSE, SPECIAL OPERATIONS/LOW–INTENSITY CONFLICT, PERFORMING THE DUTIES OF UNDER SECRETARY OF DEFENSE FOR POLICY, DEPARTMENT OF DEFENSE

Mr. LUMPKIN. Chairman Wilson, Ranking Member Davis, distinguished members of the subcommittee, thank you for your steadfast support for our service members and civilians who are missing from our Nation's past conflicts and their families who wait for news of their loved ones.

I respectfully request my written testimony be included for the record. The authorities and the appropriations that Congress has provided the Department of Defense have allowed us to continue to recover the remains of our fallen service members and provide answers to their families.

From Dr. Miller's departure in early January to late June, when Christine Wormuth was confirmed as Under Secretary of Defense, in addition to serving as the Assistant Secretary of Defense for Special Operations and Low-Intensity Conflict, I also performed the duties of the Under Secretary of Defense for Policy.

In this capacity, Secretary Hagel tasked me with leading the Department's restructuring of its personnel accounting for past conflicts to more effectively account for our missing personnel and ensure their families receive timely and accurate information. The Department is committed to improving the services we provide families.

The Department of Defense conducts accounting of the personnel missing from past conflicts to record and honor the deeds and sacrifices of our service members and the civilian personnel, and the legacy of the loss endured by their families.

The missing person is the purpose behind what we do. The families are our focus and better service is our goal. The Department recognizes that we cannot recover remains in all cases. In all cases, however, we have a duty to provide designated family members the fullest possible accounting for their loved ones. Change, even for the better, is difficult.

I appreciate this committee's support for reform, and I look forward to continuing to work with you. The Secretary's decisions to change how the Department conducts personnel accounting address deficiencies in process, workplace culture, and organizational structure.

The decisions are based on dispassionate analytical assessments and informed by feedback from families and here in the U.S. Congress. Recognizing that to fulfill this commitment to the fullest possible accounting the Department of Defense must do better, in March Secretary Hagel directed sweeping changes to how the Department of Defense operates in this area. His decision was based on careful consideration reviewed from GAO and from CAPE, independent assessments, comments from DOD Inspector General, veterans service organizations, families, and the workforce.

Secretary Hagel directed the establishment of a new defense agency that combines the functions of the DPMO, the Joint POW/MIA Accounting Command, select functions of the Air Force Life Science Equipment Laboratory. He directed that an Armed Forces medical examiner will be the single identification authority, making the process for past and current identifications the same, and overseas scientific operations in the new agency. The Department will work with Congress to realign funds for this mission into a single budget allowing for greater flexibility and availability to respond more effectively.

To improve the search, recovery, and identification process, the Department will implement a centralized database and case management system containing all missing service personnel's information. The Department is also exploring options to make this data more easily and readily available to families.

Importantly, Secretary Hagel directed the Department to develop proposals for expanding public-private partnerships in identifying our missing to leverage the capabilities of organizations outside of government that responsibly work to account for our missing.

Consolidating the organizations that work on past conflict personnel accounting is necessary, but not singularly sufficient for change we seek for families of our missing service members.

The culture of personnel accounting and processes must change as well. The Secretary's decision to increase public-private partnership, make a medical examiner the identification authority and director of scientific functions, and focus on families as the customer, are emblematic of the cultural and process changes that we are seeking to achieve.

Some of these decisions, particularly on the role of the medical examiner, are significant departures for how we have done business in the past. Implementation will require continued support for change from within the Department and from Congress. These decisions, however, are deliberate and backed by years of solid analysis from within the government and independent bodies.

To build on our strengths and change for the cultures, structures, and processes, we must take a rational approach, not one based on emotion, personal agendas, or bias. The Department will sustain and further develop the strengths of our past conflict accounting processes, notably, scientific independence and validity.

The Secretary of Defense has a longstanding personal interest in this important mission, and feels compelled to improve the Department's operations and how we support it. I have welcomed the time I spent working on this noble mission and have appreciated working with the committee and others in Congress to more effectively account for our missing personnel and ensure their families receive timely and accurate information.

I do thank you for your continued support and look forward to your questions.

[The prepared statement of Mr. Lumpkin can be found in the Appendix on page 32.]

Mr. WILSON. Thank you, Mr. Lumpkin. We will now recess and when we return, we will have a 5-minute questioning period. I want to thank in particular Craig Greene who will be monitoring 5 minutes. He himself has been a great resource working with just great capability on the issues of POW/MIA, so we're very fortunate to have Craig Greene for everyone to call on.

We are in recess.

[Recess.]

Mr. WILSON. Ladies and gentlemen, I would like to call the Subcommittee on Military Personnel of the House Armed Services back to order relative to issues of POW/MIA.

We now will begin with questions from persons, indeed we have been joined by Congressman Rich Nugent of Florida, delighted to have him here. And I will begin first.

First, again, Craig Greene will be maintaining the time, including me.

I would like to point out that one of the most meaningful experiences I have had in serving in Congress is to visit a recovery site 40 miles outside of Hue in Vietnam to see the dedication of the personnel, American and Vietnamese, for the recovery of remains of two pilots on an F–4A on the side of a hillside which went down, which is very inspiring to me, and I just want that to be the case.

Equally though, I was concerned the letter by Congressman Glenn Thompson, he has a report here that we will be giving to you, and I hope there is a response back, concerning the case of Major Lewis P. Smith III, who is missing in a plane crash in Laos and he was—the site was on a list for recovery, but in the meantime, a dam has been built. And the waters of the dam now cover the site. Certainly to me, that should have been an issue that should have given expedited interest for the recovery, but we will have this letter for you and for the family of Major Smith. I would really like to see your response.

So at this time, Mr. Lumpkin, before making your recommendation to the Secretary, how much consensus did you have among the accounting community? And how has the Department—has the Department finished the implementation plan? And if so, do you have a copy of the implementation plan?

Mr. LUMPKIN. Thank you very much for the question. As we were doing the initial assessment based on when tasked by the Secretary in looking at both the GAO report, the CAPE report, as well as numerous meetings with veterans service organizations, families, members of this committee and staff, and over on the Senate as well, I would say that it was unanimous consent that change was needed. And we worked through the different issues and proposals and socialized the potential possibilities for change and where change was needed and the important aspects that need to be changed.

I think that the most important piece that we came to conclusion, and this is kind of a business perspective, is that who is the customer here? And the customer was realized that we hadn't been focused on the families as much as we could. And so, what we have done is we have realigned. I think that was the central theme that everybody that was absolutely could get behind, was that we need to focus on the families as the customer because the missing service member can't speak for their case.

And because of the deep concern with the families, I think that is the underlying piece that everybody agreed upon. And then how we built it and the way to organize and make the recommendations. There was general consent, and some of them we had to work through. But I would say generally there was consent across the board.

Now, as far as the timeline and what that plan looks like, we had 30 days to put together what needed to be changed, and now we are figuring out some of the mechanics of how. The implementation plan is not completed as of yet. I will tell you it is broken into three different principal phases. The first is unifying the mission set for the agency, the single agency as we consolidate these different pieces. The second piece is the process. The one thing as I mentioned in my opening statement is that we need to focus on is a singular process for all cases of those that are missing and unaccounted.

And then the final piece is the people and how we are going to properly align the people in order to support the mission, because we have a tremendous and highly skilled workforce that is passionate about this mission. And we need to make sure we remove those barriers that have impeded them from being successful, largely bureaucratic barriers. Secretary Hagel is adamant about cutting bureaucracy whenever possible and enabling the accounting community team to do the mission at hand.

So our timelines that we are looking at, is we are looking at an initial operating capability of a new agency, at the beginning—January 1st, 2015, and to have a fully operational capable agency on January 1st, 2016. This may seem like a protracted timeline, but some of these changes do require, in order to create the single agency, are legislative. We have to realign budgets within and we have to realign the workforce, and that takes time to do.

That said, while we are focused on rebuilding and reconstituting—the accounting community, it is essentially like flying an airplane while you are building it, because we are not going to cease doing the mission today. So we are going to continue to do the mission today while we are creating this new accounting agency.

Mr. WILSON. This is very encouraging, as you say change needed, that is impressive to me without recrimination and apparently, hopefully, without turf protection. And I want to thank you for addressing the issues of fragmentation.

And indeed, Dr. Morin, the funding for this with the constraints on Department of Defense and the issue, particularly of sequestration, what is the status of funding?

Dr. MORIN. So Mr. Chairman, I would divide the status of funding into two pieces. The first is the administrative or clerical task of realigning the streams of funding. Right? So we will be standing up an individual organization that will bring together multiple organizations. It needs to have its own concrete, coherent stream of funding. The DOD Comptroller and my staff are working that issue to ensure that when that organization becomes operationally capable, it has got the line on the resources it needs from an administrative perspective. They also need support in areas of contracting and financial management and all of the other administrative areas necessary for them to be successful. So we are working that piece.

The second question is just how many resources are applied to this mission. As you know, this is a mission where the Department has invested significant resources. The Department added additional resources after the enactment of the 200 accounted-for per year goal. Didn't see very much in the way of return in terms of additional identifications. Obviously each identification is its own case, with its own details. Some come comparatively easy; others are the product of many, many years of work.

But what we need to do, in my estimation and the estimation of the CAPE team, is focus on implementing the reorganization and the reforms that are laid out in the reports and the action proposal that Mr. Lumpkin has put together, and then assess whether that streamlined and more effective organization is able to deliver sufficient capability, sufficient identification, sufficient service to the families, in order to be deemed successful or whether the Secretary needs to add additional financial and human resources to get there. We simply don't know how efficient that redesigned organization will be until we have given them a chance to stand up.

Mr. WILSON. Thank you very much. Keep us informed in however we can be of assistance.

Ranking Member Susan Davis of California.

Mrs. DAVIS. Thank you, Mr. Chairman. Welcome to both of you.

Secretary Lumpkin, could you please within that timeframe you talked about, the 15 to 16, the initial work and then after 16 to be at full capacity, could you give us a little bit more detail about what that is going to look like within that initial phase, initial year? And do you need any additional authorities to accomplish this effort overall? Do you anticipate that?

Mr. LUMPKIN. The Congress thus far, and this committee in particular, has been very supportive, with Representative Nugent championing the amendment for the midstream legislative proposal to support this realignment has been the first step for us to get things moving forward.

We are also looking at a reprogramming right now for this fiscal year of funds, unobligated funds to go against this new agency. This is important for many reasons, because we are going to have expenses that occur in support of standing this organization, this new agency, up, but it also is a shot across the bow to all in the Department of Defense that we are at a point where we can't turn back, nor are we going to turn back. It is symbolic of the Secretary's commitment that we are with going to get this done and we are going to get it done right.

So, as we move forward, those are the initial steps that we have taken in order to get to the initial operating capability of 1 January.

What we have done, is we have assigned a senior executive, Ms. Alyssa Stack, and she is working as the program executive officer full-time to support and build this realignment and restructuring of the accounting community. So she is building, she has a team that she has been given, she has been given resources, we have brought on contract support, we have brought on all—and given her the tools necessary to flesh out a complete schedule on what the timeline in order to make that fully operational capability of 1 January 2016.

And I would propose that quarterly, at a minimum, I come up and talk to you all and to keep you updated and the next—at the first opportunity to lay that plan out when it is completed, and then Alyssa and myself or a representative would come up and talk to you and walk you and to keep the in-progress reviews as we move through, because I value your insight as we move forward and get this restructured.

We have an opportunity that doesn't happen very often when you are in a program and that is to do kind of a control, alt, delete, and reset. We have the opportunity to do this, and this is the Secretary's commitment is do it, do it right, do it well, and do it once.

Mrs. DAVIS. Thank you. So you are not—really feel in a position to give us a little bit more of what is in that, but to bring it forward.

Mr. LUMPKIN. I would like a little more time, just to—so I can put it in a nice tight, crisp package for you and answer all your questions so we are not creating more for you.

Mrs. DAVIS. Thank you. Dr. Morin, we know the tight budget situation. There probably are—hopefully there will be a few instances with the consolidation where we gain some efficiencies, but on the other hand, you are going to need more money possibly.

I guess what I am wondering is how you might protect some of these different funds that we are trying to bring together as we go through some more difficult budget cuts. How do you think that is going to play out?

Dr. MORIN. Absolutely, Mrs. Davis. I think that is a critical question for the Department. Mr. Lumpkin referenced the reprogramming, so on behalf of my former colleagues in the comptroller world, that is a package that has just come to the Congress now a couple of days ago. There is $2.5 million in there requested to initiate activity in the new agency; prompt approval of that will let the process begin. So we would certainly appreciate that.

Looking at the overall resource picture, just to keep the magnitude in your mind, this is—in recent years has been a $100 million-plus-per-year enterprise. So not a trivial commitment of taxpayer dollars, but not a trivial debt owed to the families of those who were lost in the—soldier, sailor, airmen, and marines who are still carried on the rolls as missing. But we do certainly have a clear obligation to stewardship here.

So that is where I would like to give the work that Mr. Lumpkin's plan has laid out a chance to work and see how it works, and at that point, assess where the resource shortfalls are.

The Department, back in the fiscal 2012 budget submission, applied very significant additional resources to this enterprise, taking it from what was typically a $60- to $70 million-a-year undertaking to, you know, well over $100 million. And so, some of those dollars were lost to that enterprise as a result of Budget Control Act reductions, headquarters staff reductions and the like. And some of it frankly, you know, for example, in the case of JPAC, the Pacific Command assessed that given the challenges there and the fact that hiring freezes were in place, that they wouldn't be able to spend those resources and so reductions were made in the year of execution to respond to the crisis of sequestration.

No question that those things have had an impact on the ability of the community to deliver. Again, our assessment is the bulk of the problem was an organizational structure that needed addressing.

Mrs. DAVIS. Thank you.

Mr. WILSON. Thank you, Ms. Davis. We now proceed to Congressman Walter Jones of North Carolina.

Mr. JONES. Mr. Chairman, thank you very much. Mr. Lumpkin, I listened intently, or carefully, maybe is a better word, to you and the doctor's comments. And mine is going to deal primarily with the comment you made about we realize that we need to strengthen—maybe that is my word, the public-private partnership.

A few years ago I was contacted by Mark Noah, who is the person that put together History Flight. And Mark came to me because he was having trouble getting information from JPAC, and we were able to intercede, working with the Department of Defense to help him have access to records.

He has—his organization since 2010, and it is a private organization, has 117 total identifications. In the year of 2014 alone, he has already 36 recoveries to date. I know you are talking about reorganization and hopefully making for more efficiency because of the families and the loved ones that never came home, but he is saying to me that for his recoveries it costs an average of $150,000, where when the Federal Government goes out to recover, it is somewhere around $1 million.

I hope that Secretary Hagel, who I have great respect for, that you will look seriously at these entities like History Flight who have a reputation, who, in many ways, is doing a much better job than the Federal Government. And I would hope that we would learn from these private entities who are making such impressive recoveries at their own expense.

I will tell you, I have never met a person more committed than Mark Noah to recovering these family—for these families, their loss of loved ones. I mean he flies for Federal Express, these are his monies. I don't think he gets any reimbursement nor do I think he has asked for any from the Department of Defense. I would like to hear your comment, because on the fact that these—the part of public partnership is going to be strengthened, because to me, we are losing a valuable asset that could help these families bring home their loved ones and bring that sad chapter to an end. I would like to hear your comment on these private entities, specifically my comments about History Flight.

Mr. LUMPKIN. Thank you, sir. I have met Mark Noah numerous times. He and I are in regular contact. I have solicited his input as well as that of other private organizations on how they do business and where we can find opportunities to work together.

So please understand that I have personally sat down with Mark on numerous occasions to find out how he is doing business and how we can partner to work together, both government and History Flight as a private organization, and organizations like History Flight, in order to bring home those that are missing.

So, he has been integral to our public-private venture. And largely, he has a very good and robust investigative arm as well as an excavation piece that he does. But there are other organizations very similar that do it with great acumen and we are working with them to make sure we can get the relationships codified and the requirements, both safety requirements on the site, get the proper permits done, and sure we can repatriate remains in a proper fashion and all of the things that go into it.

Some of those costs that the U.S. Government bears, whether History of Flight does the excavation or DOD does the excavation.

So absolutely, I hear you loud and clear. And he is one of those people that we are talking to and we see as a partner.

Mr. JONES. Mr. Lumpkin, probably some time as we move forward, I would appreciate it, maybe in September if you—that my office contacts you that you could come to my office and kind of give us an update and a briefing on these relationships, because I think in this tight budget time, that if we can come together and find the remains, but also to cut the costs, which may allow this government to even do more for the families. I understand—very quickly, I know my time is up, but there are currently about 78,000 missing World War II veterans and about 16,000 missing from the Vietnam war. And if we don't start to really make a commitment and it has to be from outside sources working with you in the leadership role, let me make that clear, which I would support, then I think we are missing a great opportunity to do God's work. Thank you.

Mr. LUMPKIN. I would welcome the opportunity to come brief you in September or whenever is convenient for you. Please understand that as we are looking to build to the capacity of 200 identifications a year, the public-private partnerships are part of the strategy to get to that capacity.

Mr. JONES. Thank you, sir. Thank you, Mr. Chairman.

Mr. WILSON. Thank you very much, Mr. Jones. We now proceed to Congressman Austin Scott of Georgia.

Mr. SCOTT. Thank you, Mr. Chairman. I would like to follow up too on what my friend, Mr. Jones, was talking about. We have widely accepted that it is over 80,000 service members. The number Mr. Jones just gave was right at 94,000. What number are you comfortable with as far as the unaccounted for? What do you believe that number——

Mr. LUMPKIN. I believe the operating number is in the vicinity of 83,000 that are unaccounted for. Please understand that a vast majority of those are realistically not recoverable, lost at sea. And so as we look at this in the future, we have to categorize people, the missing, accordingly so we are putting the resources against those that are cases.

Mr. SCOTT. Of the 83,000, we certainly understand that in these horrible situations somebody lost at sea that may never be recovered, how many do you believe are recoverable?

Mr. LUMPKIN. I have seen estimations between 19- and 28,000 are deemed to be effectively recoverable.

Mr. SCOTT. Let's use 25,000, kind of in the middle there. If we do 200 a year, that is 125 years. I think that is where, as we move forward—and I certainly appreciate your willingness to work with private sectors, again, my friend Mr. Jones was talking about, but that is just too long. My grandfather was a POW in World War II, he made it home, fortunately; some of his friends didn't, some of the people that were on the plane with him when it went down didn't. But if we just do the math, simple math that comes out to 125 years. So any way we can bring in the private sector is something I think that we have to do so that these families can get closure on this issue.

As we go forward I know the recovery, and the lab work, the repatriation, all of these things will have to continue as we go through the restructuring. Are you confident that you have the framework in place so that there is not a disruption in the process of the recovery while these changes move forward over the next several months?

Mr. LUMPKIN. I believe we have the framework. I think we have built the framework and then we have the commitment of the Secretary who has made his guidance very clear to the defense enterprise that this is going to happen. So all are on board, so I feel that we have the tools necessary to continue operations while we stand up this new agency.

Mr. SCOTT. How long do you expect it to take to stand up the new agency? When do you expect and when do you expect it to be completed?

Mr. LUMPKIN. We expect initial operational capability on 1 January 2015, and then fully operational on 1 January 2016.

Mr. SCOTT. While this is happening, who will handle the current recovery and lab work and repatriation?

Mr. LUMPKIN. JPAC, which is the Joint POW/MIA Accounting Command in Hawaii, will continue to do its mission as currently stated. And the Defense Prisoner of War/Missing in Action Office here in Washington, DC, will continue to do their job, and the Life Science Equipment Lab in its current structure will do its job.

So we are building something up while we are shrinking those capabilities down to make sure that it is seamless.

Mr. SCOTT. Thanks for those answers. I, again, want to go back and reiterate the point if we have 25,000 missing in action that are recoverable, and we only retrieve—only achieve 200 a year in returning them to their families, that that is 125 years. And that is— any way we can bring the private sector in and others to help us increase that pace is something that I hope you will continue to work with us on.

Thank you, Mr. Chairman, I yield back the remainder of my time.

Mr. WILSON. Thank you, Congressman Scott. We now proceed to Congressman Rich Nugent of Florida.

Mr. NUGENT. Thank you, Mr. Chairman, and thank you for allowing me to be here today in this setting. I want to thank both Dr. Morin and Mr. Lumpkin in regards to how you are moving forward. I think you are using a very deliberate approach in regards to getting this transitional person in there early, to start laying out where you are trying to go. I am not going to really ask any specific questions just because it is so early in the process. I do appreciate, Mr. Lumpkin, your willingness to come back here on a quarterly basis to apprise us as to how this process is moving along.

And I just think any time you can merge two organizations together, I mean, there is going to be some hiccups along the way. It sounds like you are going to be able to continue to do the job that is necessary to do within the next, a little over a year, but I would—I guess my question falls along where Mr. Scott was going with 25,000-plus that we think are recoverable and that you really did push that number out 125 years. Most families wouldn't even know—there is such a distance between the date of death, the missing to come up.

How do you prioritize in regards to going out to locate remains to bring them back and give them the proper honors they deserve? How do we prioritize that?

Mr. LUMPKIN. It is an interesting question because it is an evolving process, as you are aware, prior to 2010, recovering those missing from World War II were not part of the Department of Defense's mission set. So that was through legislation that was created. So we had a number of 65,000-plus that were added virtually overnight. So from 2010, we have restructured and we have relooked at how to do business is to focus on—because you have multiple kind of lines of effort, and they are frequently based on conflict. In the sense that Southeast Asia, for example, there has been numerous decades of work and research done to build the intelligence and the information in order to where to go in order to do an excavation to recover the remains. So we have very mature case files.

North Korea, and Korea, for example, North Korea there are significant access problems currently which makes it difficult for us to work in the field on those particular cases. In World War II now, since it has been added to our mission set, we are spending a large part of the effort building the case files to get the intelligence and the information of where those missing are actually at. And this is where many of those in the private sector have been working these issues for years, and have done a lot of research that we can build on.

So maybe I am being optimistic here, and I like to be optimistic and plan for it, but I believe that we are going to see a period of time if we open up effectively our public-private partnership, we will see the opportunities with regard to identifying those missing from World War II increase significantly as we are able to increase our capabilities of research on that effort and working with public-private in that forum in order to harness all the great work they have done in the research and to build the case files. I am very optimistic that we will build to capacity significantly in the coming years.

Mr. NUGENT. I think it is great.

Mr. LUMPKIN. If I may just finish, I said in my opening comments is that change even for the better is painful, it is difficult.

Mr. NUGENT. It always is.

Mr. LUMPKIN. It is. Over the years, because where we have gone is that we built the accounting community by bolting a piece on, bolting a piece on there, and it has built into this thing. All great people working hard to get the mission done, but I think that is why we are here at this point of where it is a natural inflection point for reorganization.

Mr. NUGENT. And hopefully, as you do move along this reorganization is that one component or at least somebody is given the responsibility to work with those nongovernment organizations to get more bang for our buck. The whole idea is not about—to me it is not about the dollars, it is about bringing these folks back home.

Mr. LUMPKIN. Absolutely. And closure for the families, because they are the center of this when it is all said and done.

Mr. NUGENT. Absolutely. So I would hope that that is part of the equation, have somebody that is responsible for and is accountable for working with those groups to get more access.

Mr. LUMPKIN. It is.

Mr. NUGENT. I appreciate it. Thank you very, very much for your comments. I yield back.

Mr. WILSON. Thank you, Congressman Nugent. We would like to thank both of you for being here today. Again, we are all very appreciative of the competence and capabilities and the dedication of the people who are working on these issues. And I want to join with Congressman Nugent, too, to wish you well as they are merged, in the interest, again, of our veterans and military families and current service members too.

There being no further business, we are adjourned.

[Whereupon, at 3:46 p.m., the subcommittee was adjourned.]

APPENDIX

JULY 15, 2014

PREPARED STATEMENTS SUBMITTED FOR THE RECORD

JULY 15, 2014

Chairman Wilson Opening Statement
Government Accountability Office Review of the Prisoner of War/Missing in Action (POW/MIA) Community and the Restructuring of These Agencies as Proposed by the Department of Defense
15 July 2014

The hearing will come to order. I would like to welcome everyone to the Subcommittee on Military Personnel as we hear from witnesses on the planned reorganization of the POW/MIA Accounting Community of the Department of Defense. Almost a year ago this subcommittee held a hearing on GAO's report on their review of the Department's efforts to meet the 2010 mandate to identify 200 missing persons per year by 2015 and Dr. Paul Cole's report titled "JPAC's Information Value Chain—The Identification of Missing Persons". The GAO report and I hope our committee's interest and oversight of this issue became what I believe is a catalyst for change. Reviews by the office of the Cost Assessment and Program Evaluation and the Office of the Inspector General began shortly after our hearing and on 31 March 2014 Secretary Hagel announced the reorganization of the accounting community based on the recommendations of the reviews. Today, the subcommittee will continue its oversight on this important issue to hear from our witnesses on how they came to the conclusions and recommendations announced by the Secretary and the way ahead for the reorganization of the POW/MIA Accounting Community.

The men and women, both in uniform and DOD civilian personnel, who perform this mission are very dedicated to this effort and have done incredible work in the past. I am confident that they will continue as professionals as the Department moves forward with these efforts. I am anxious to move forward with this endeavor as I firmly believe that we, as a nation, owe the proper emphasis, resources and priority of effort to account for our missing persons from past conflicts and to bring closure to their family members.

I would like to welcome our distinguished witnesses:

Dr. Jamie Morin, (Newly confirmed) Director, Cost Assessment and Program Evaluation (CAPE), Department of Defense

Mr. Michael D. Lumpkin, Assistant Secretary of Defense, Special Operations / Low-Intensity Conflict (ASD SO/LIC), Performing the Duties of Under Secretary of Defense for Policy, Department of Defense

STATEMENT FOR THE RECORD

HONORABLE JAMIE M. MORIN

DIRECTOR COST ASSESSMENT AND PROGRAM EVALUATION

BEFORE THE 113th CONGRESS

HOUSE ARMED SERVICES COMMITTEE

MILITARY PERSONNEL SUBCOMMITTEE

JULY 15, 2014

Chairman Wilson, Ranking Member Davis, thank you for your continued commitment to ensuring that families of service members who remain missing from our nation's conflicts get the answers they need. The Department of Defense is able to seek and recover the remains of our fallen heroes, and bring closure for the families, thanks to the authorities and appropriations that Congress has provided. We appreciate the Committee's continued engagement on this challenging issue.

The Department has a solemn duty to provide the families of the fallen with the fullest possible accounting of their loved ones. In 2009, Congress passed legislation requiring the Department to increase its personnel accounting capacity in order to account for at least 200 missing personnel annually beginning in FY 2015, but despite a strong commitment from leadership, when CAPE assessed progress since the legislation it was clear that fundamental reform was required to put us on a path to achieve this goal. In my testimony today, I will update the committee on the steps that CAPE recommended in order to reform an imperfect system and thereby better honor the sacrifices made by our service members and their families.

As this committee is very much aware, in July 2013, the Government Accountability Office (GAO) issued a report stating that a fragmented organizational structure undermined DoD's ability to accomplish its missing persons accounting mission. In response to this report, then-Deputy Secretary of Defense Ashton B. Carter tasked CAPE to do 4 things:

1. assess the current structure of the personnel accounting community and determine if the structure is effective and cost efficient;

2. determine how various components of the personnel accounting community support the identification process;

3. evaluate whether the 200 accounted-for goal is the optimal metric; and

4. provide recommendations for alternative organizational structures and processes to conduct the mission effectively.

Our study confirmed and expanded on many of the findings in the GAO report. In testimony today, I will highlight the four main recommendations of our study. We should

1. Fundamentally reform the organizational structure of the personnel accounting community;

2. Add a Medical Examiner as the lead authority for establishing a formal identification;

3. Re-scope the activities of the Central Identification Laboratory (CIL); and

4. Complement the total number of identifications goal with a broader range of appropriate metrics reflecting the full range of efforts initiated and executed by the DoD Accounting Community.

Organizational Structure

One of the key findings of the CAPE review is that the past-conflict accounting mission is complicated by the fact that it is conducted by so many organizations in DoD, including:

- the Defense Prisoner of War/Missing Personnel Office (DPMO);

- the Joint POW/MIA Accounting Command (JPAC);

- the Armed Forces DNA Identification Laboratory (AFDIL);

- the Life Sciences Equipment Laboratory (LSEL); and

- the Service Casualty Offices (SCOs).

Simply reading this long list of agencies and acronyms begins to convey how complex the personnel accounting system is. As both GAO and our study made clear, there is no single office or individual responsible for leading the accounting effort. The absence of a single, accountable individual has resulted in duplication of effort among organizations, which has driven inefficiencies and institutional conflict. Specific areas of duplication and inefficiency include:

- negotiations with other countries,

- research and analysis,

- life science equipment analysis,

- support staff,

- external communications, and

- contracting for genealogical histories.

In addition, numerous institutional conflicts within and among organizations in the community have led to mistrust, dysfunction, and unproductive behavior by individuals.

After conducting interviews with 26 government offices to gain a greater understanding of the personnel accounting mission and weighing the pros and cons of multiple organizational options, CAPE recommends unification of DPMO and JPAC into a single Defense Agency with a new name. The new organization should report to the Under Secretary of Defense for Policy and be civilian-led with a 2-star military deputy. We do not recommend the consolidation of the DNA laboratory, AFDIL, because of its substantial duties unrelated to the past-conflict accounting mission. However, we do call for a process in which AFDIL and similarly situated organizations accept tasking and case prioritization from the director of the new agency when they are performing their past-conflict accounting roles.

It is important that the new agency is appropriately resourced and supported by DoD to handle all legal, contracting, and operational support issues that will arise during the conduct of the personnel accounting mission. Under the proposed organizational structure the new agency does not report through a geographic combatant command, which would provide these services to a subordinate component.

Rely on a Medical Examiner for Identifications

Another key recommendation from our study is that a medical examiner be included in the identification process and be the final DoD authority for establishing a formal identification. Incorporating a medical examiner into the process would address legal issues that have arisen concerning the movement of remains from Europe to the United States and the interstate transfer of remains within the United States. This change would also create consistency between DoD processes in place for past conflict deaths and those for current deaths.

Re-scope the Responsibilities of the Central Identification Laboratory

Second, CAPE also recommends re-scoping the activities of JPAC's Central Identification Laboratory (CIL) to focus solely on skeletal and dental remains. Significant duplication has developed in activities conducted by the CIL and other organizations in the Accounting Community. In particular, research and analysis and life science analysis functions that are carried out within other parts of JPAC, DPMO, and LSEL, are also present in the CIL. Re-scoping the CIL to focus solely on skeletal and dental analysis would reduce redundancies, capitalize on specialization, and refine division of labor

Metrics

Dr. Carter also tasked CAPE to evaluate whether the "200 accounted-for goal is the optimal metric." The National Defense Authorization Act (NDAA) for FY 2010 directs DoD to increase the capacity of the personnel accounting community to ensure that at least 200 missing persons are accounted for each year beginning in FY 2015. In FY 2013, DoD accounted for 60 personnel. While the reorganization proposals that come out of our report should help to accelerate the work of the accounting community, CAPE assesses that the Department is unlikely to achieve the 200 annual accounted-for goal on a sustained basis, even with increased resources.

Developing appropriate management metrics for complicated enterprises is a tough undertaking, so I did want to note some of the issues associated with using 200-accounted-for per year as the primary benchmark for evaluating the accounting community's performance. The focus on absolute quantity of new identifications incentivizes the personnel accounting community to seek easier cases. It is likely to lead to an increase in disinterment and recovery missions, focused on WWII and Korea cases, which yield a higher probability of success and higher numbers of remains than more difficult missions associated with comparatively well-searched areas like

South East Asia. This will help to bring closure to more families, but also a higher percentage of older cases.

Second, the fact that only new identifications count toward the statutory metric deemphasizes important efforts by the CIL and AFDIL to determine whether previously unidentified remains are part of the remains of individuals who have already been identified. Such efforts are necessary, especially for cases involving co-mingled remains. The results of these activities are not currently captured in the statutory accounted-for metric.

Finally, a focus on the number of those who are annually accounted for as the only metric to be applied to the efforts of the DoD accounting community is too limited to reflect the output of the personnel accounting community in caring for the families of the fallen. It fails to consider the full range of efforts of the community, especially areas like historical and outreach work to inform relatives about the fate of their family members. The Department puts a significant amount of effort into this work, and continues to believe that it is an important part of the overall personnel accounting agenda.

In response to these issues, CAPE recommends the accounting community adopt and report a more diversified portfolio of output metrics – going beyond those required by statute – reflecting the full range of effort initiated and executed by the DoD personnel accounting community. A list of possible metrics for consideration is provided in the report. These include: the number of primary next of kin and other family notifications representing new information about the missing service member, the number of actionable new leads, and the number of missions executed and sites excavated.

Regardless of the specific metrics applied, DoD must improve transparency and reporting to the families, the public, and Congress on the personnel accounting mission. Perhaps most significantly, DoD must improve public awareness that the remains of as many as half of the unaccounted-for personnel are likely to never be recovered, primarily because they were lost at sea in ship sinkings or airplane crashes (the vast majority are from World War II).

Several members of Congress believe that an improved level of transparency is necessary in this mission area. For example, Senators McCaskill and Ayotte's January 10, 2014 letter to the Secretary of Defense states, "It is time that families are given honest answers about the chances of their loved ones being found, identified, and brought home." Also, the FY 2014 NDAA required the DoD to report to Congress on the number of missing persons considered unrecoverable.

To address these concerns, we recommend that the accounting community categorize cases for all conflicts as either active pursuit cases or non-recoverable, and inform family members of the case status that applies to their loved ones.

Finally, CAPE also identified a number of improvements for each of the personnel accounting organizations that were included in this review. They include: publishing a new DoD Directive that specifically addresses the new organization's roles, responsibilities, and interactions with other components of the accounting community; annual reporting requirements; instituting consistent policies and practices for annual events for all family members of missing service members, regardless of the conflict in which they served; and establishing a standard case management tool, or database, that is accessible, with appropriate restrictions and controls, to all parts of the accounting community, including families. These changes, along with others identified in the report, should be implemented to improve business practices and mission effectiveness throughout the community.

Conclusion

In their report last year, the GAO stated that "Top-Level Leadership Attention [is] Needed" to address the personnel accounting issues. My assessment is that is exactly what has happened. The CAPE study team has presented its findings to Secretary Hagel. Those findings informed the Secretary's decisions to reorganize the community and improve business processes. Subsequently, the Deputy Secretary asked Assistant Secretary Lumpkin to return in August with an implementation plan to achieve initial and final operating capabilities for the new agency along with other major milestones. Mr Lumpkin will lay out his plan in detail.

Chairman Wilson and Ranking Member Davis, you stated in your September 3, 2013, letter to the Secretary of Defense that you were not satisfied with the status quo. The Secretary is not satisfied either. The Department is duty-bound to honor the service of our fallen service members and to ensure that their families are provided with timely, accurate information about their loved ones.

Thank you for your continued support concerning this important mission. In closing, I would like to pass on my thanks to the CAPE staff who performed this study and who carried it through to conclusion even before my arrival. They did great work with the support and involvement of other players from throughout the personnel accouning community. They are committed to continued involvement to support Mr Lumpkin's reform effort and are actively participating in his implementation team.

Dr. Jamie M. Morin
Director, Cost Assessment and Program Evaluation

Jamie Morin was confirmed by the Senate as the second Director of Cost Assessment and
Program Evaluation for the Department of Defense on June 25, 2014.
As director, he leads an organization responsible for analyzing and
evaluating the Department's plans, programs, and budgets in relation to
U.S. defense objectives, projected threats, allied contributions,
estimated costs, and resource constraints. The CAPE organization
continues the heritage of the Systems Analysis office created by
Secretary Robert McNamara and later renamed as Program Analysis
and Evaluation. To support better defense decision making, CAPE
develops analytical tools and methods for analyzing national security
planning and the allocation of resources, and ensures that the costs of
DoD programs are properly estimated and presented accurately.

Prior to joining CAPE, Morin served for five years as the Assistant Secretary of the Air Force for
Financial Management and Comptroller. As the Air Force's chief financial officer, he was the
principal advisor to the Secretary and Chief of Staff of the Air Force on financial matters,
responsible for the financial and analytical services necessary for the effective and efficient use of
Air Force resources. This included directing the development of the Air Force budget, overseeing
the Air Force Cost Analysis Agency and conducting Air Force accounting and finance operations.

From July 3, 2012 until April 29, 2013, he was appointed by the President as Acting Under
Secretary of the Air Force, during which time he served as the service's chief management
officer, senior energy official, chair of the Air Force Space Board, and acting Secretary of the Air
Force during absences of the Secretary.

From 2003 until 2009, Morin was a member of the professional staff of the U.S. Senate
Committee on the Budget, serving as the committee's lead analyst for the defense, intelligence,
and foreign affairs budgets, responsible for drafting relevant sections of the congressional budget
resolution and advising the Senate on enforcement of budget rules.

Earlier in his career, Morin served in the Office of the Under Secretary of Defense for Policy and
as an economic development strategist with the firm J.E. Austin Associates. His academic
research focused on U.S. national security policy, particularly the role of Congress in defense
budgeting and policy making. He held fellowships at the University of Virginia's Miller Center
for Public Affairs and at the Center for Strategic and Budgetary Assessments, where he
conducted research for the Pentagon's Office of Net Assessment. He also served as a policy
advisor on President Obama's defense transition team.

STATEMENT FOR THE RECORD

HONORABLE MICHAEL D. LUMPKIN

ASSISTANT SECRETARY OF DEFENSE

SPECIAL OPERATIONS AND LOW INTENSITY CONFLICT

BEFORE THE 113th CONGRESS

HOUSE ARMED SERVICES COMMITTEE

MILITARY PERSONNEL SUBCOMMITTEE

JULY 15, 2014

Introduction

Chairman Wilson, Ranking Member Davis, distinguished members of the subcommittee, thank you for your steadfast support for our service members who are missing from our nation's past conflicts and their families who wait for news of their loved ones. The authorities and appropriations the Congress has provided to the Department of Defense have allowed us to continue to recover the remains of our fallen heroes and to provide answers to their families.

From Dr. Jim Miller's departure in early January to late June, when Ms. Christine Wormuth was confirmed as the Under Secretary of Defense for Policy, in addition to serving as the Assistant Secretary of Defense for Special Operations and Low Intensity Conflict, I also performed the duties of the Under Secretary of Defense for Policy. In this capacity, Secretary Hagel tasked me with leading the Department's restructuring of its personnel accounting for past conflicts to account for our missing personnel more effectively and to ensure that their families receive timely and accurate information. The Department is committed to improving the services we provide families.

The Department of Defense conducts accounting of personnel missing from past conflicts to record and honor the deeds and sacrifices of our service members, civilian personnel, and the legacy of loss endured by their families. Locating and identifying the missing person is the mission. Their families are our focus, and better service to those families is our goal. The Department recognizes that we cannot recover remains in all cases, but we have a duty to provide designated family members the fullest possible accounting of their loved ones.

Change, even for the better, can be difficult. I appreciate this Committee's support for reform and I look forward to continuing to work with you. The Secretary's decisions to change how the Department conducts personnel accounting address deficiencies in process, workplace culture, and organizational structure. The decisions are based on dispassionate analytical assessments and informed by feedback from families and Congress.

Government Accountability Office Study

As the committee is aware, the Secretary decided to restructure how the Department conducts personnel accounting after careful consideration of reviews by the Government Accountability Office (GAO) and by the Office of Cost Assessment and Program Evaluation (CAPE), and of independent assessments and comments from the DoD Inspector General, veterans' service organizations, families of the missing, and the workforce. This Committee, in fact, directed the GAO review in the summer of 2012 to examine the processes and structure of the personnel accounting community.

The GAO found that the Department had not completed a plan to meet the requirements and goals set by Congress in the Fiscal Year 2010 National Defense Authorization Act, and that the personnel accounting community's fragmented organizational structure undermined the Department's capability and capacity to accomplish its mission. The GAO made the following nine recommendations to improve the Department's personnel accounting effort:

- Examine options for reorganization.

- Clarify roles and responsibilities in four key functional areas:

  o equipment and artifact identification and analysis;

  o research and analysis;

  o investigations; and

  o family outreach and external communications.

- Develop a new memorandum of agreement between the Life Sciences Equipment Laboratory (LSEL) and the Joint Prisoner of War/Missing in Action (POW/MIA) Accounting Command (JPAC).

- Finalize the Department's community-wide plan to develop the increased capability and capacity required by applicable statute.

- Establish criteria that can be used to prioritize recovery efforts.

- Establish a mechanism for community-wide communication.

- Formalize JPAC and Service Casualty Officer communication procedures.

- Develop personnel files for all unaccounted persons as required by statute.

- Develop memorandums of agreement between the Commander, U.S. Pacific Command, and the Commander, JPAC, and other geographic Combatant Commands.

The Department accepted all nine recommendations made by the GAO and has implemented three of them: examine options for re-organization, develop a memorandum of agreement between LSEL and JPAC, and formalize JPAC and Service casualty office communications procedures. The remaining recommendations are in various stages of completion and will be incorporated into the plan to restructure the personnel accounting community.

Cost Assessment and Program Evaluation Office (CAPE) Study

Also, last summer, at the request of the then-Under Secretary of Defense for Policy, Dr. Jim Miller, the Deputy Secretary of Defense tasked the Director of the Cost Assessment and Program Evaluation Office (CAPE) to:

- Assess the current structure of the personnel accounting community and determine if it is effective and cost efficient.

- Determine how the various components of the personnel accounting community support the identification process.

- Evaluate whether or not the accounted-for goal contained in the Fiscal Year 2010 National Defense Authorization Act is the optimal metric.

– Provide recommendations for alternative organizational structures and processes to conduct this mission effectively.

CAPE completed its review in March, and I defer to my colleague Dr. Morin to address CAPE's findings in detail.

Secretary Hagel's Decision

In light of these reviews and comments from others, on February 20, 2014, Secretary Hagel determined that the Department must change the way it accounts for its personnel who are missing from past conflicts. The Secretary directed me, as Acting Under Secretary of Defense for Policy, to develop a plan for how to organize the Department most effectively to increase to the maximum extent possible the numbers of missing Service personnel accounted for annually while ensuring timely and accurate information is provided to their families. On March 25, I presented my plan to the Secretary, and he approved recommendations to restructure the community, streamline and redesign business practices, and expand services to families. Specifically, he directed that the following actions be accomplished:

- Create a new Defense Agency. The new agency will combine the resources of the Defense Prisoner of War/Missing Personnel Office (DPMO), JPAC, and select functions of LSEL, under one new Defense Agency led by a non-career member of the Senior Executive Service with a General/Flag Officer as Deputy. Establishing this new Defense Agency will improve the Department's performance in past conflict accounting by streamlining organizations and processes and refocusing our organizational culture. The new Defense Agency will be responsible for all aspects of past conflict personnel accounting, including resource management across the Department and policy for personnel recovery.

- <u>Centralize oversight under a single Principal Staff Assistant.</u> The Under Secretary of Defense for Policy (USD (P)) will have policy oversight responsibilities for personnel accounting matters and will exercise authority, direction, and control over the new Defense Agency. The Under Secretary of Defense for Personnel and Readiness (USD (P&R)) will retain oversight for the Armed Forces Medical Examiner System, and will be the principal advisor to the USD (P) on the forensic medical discipline, including laboratory and identification policy and operations.

- <u>Assign a Medical Examiner to the new Defense Agency.</u> The Assistant Secretary of Defense for Health Affairs, through the USD (P&R), will assign a medical examiner from the Armed Forces Medical Examiner System (AFMES) whose primary duties will be in support of the identification of remains from past conflicts and military operations at the new Defense Agency. AFMES will exercise Department of Defense scientific authority for past conflict identifications. The assigned Medical Examiner will oversee the scientific operations of the new Defense Agency, which will include what is today JPAC and the LSEL located in Dayton, Ohio. The AFMES and the assigned past conflicts accounting Medical Examiner will remain within Department of Defense medical channels under the direction, authority, and control of the USD (P&R) through the ASD (HA).

- <u>Establish new metrics for past conflict accounting</u>. The Department will work closely with Congress, families, and veterans' service organizations, to establish metrics for assessing past conflict accounting that identify the families as the customers and must demonstrate commitment to the process of recovery and family satisfaction.

- <u>Work with Congress to realign funds to a single budget line</u>. The Under Secretary of Defense (Comptroller) (USD (C)) and the USD (P) will develop a plan to realign funds from DPMO, JPAC, and LSEL to the new Defense Agency in this fiscal year. There are more parts of the Department involved in POW/MIA activities than these three entities; however, it may not be cost effective or efficient to combine the funding for these other entities into the new agency. The USD (C) and USD (P) will develop options for how the new Defense Agency will exercise oversight of components outside of the new Defense Agency.

- <u>Implement a single centralized database and case management system</u>. The new Defense Agency will be responsible for establishing and maintaining a centralized database and case management system containing all missing service members' information, including pertinent information regarding their cases. The database and case management system will be accessible to all elements of the Department involved in the search, recovery, identification, and communications phases of the program to account for missing personnel.

- Improve external communications and family outreach. The new Defense Agency will be responsible for managing, organizing, and working with the Service Casualty Offices (SCOs) on communication with the family members of missing personnel from past conflicts. The casualty affairs responsibilities will remain with the Secretaries of the Military Departments. The Director of the new Defense Agency, in coordination with the SCOs, will develop guidance that details roles and responsibilities to ensure responsive, timely, and transparent communications with the families. Additionally, the new Defense Agency will establish communications with veterans' service organizations (VSOs), concerned citizens, and the public on the Department's efforts to account for missing personnel. All external communications with families, VSOs, concerned citizens, and the public will be robust and two-way. All external communications and events dealing with unaccounted-for personnel in which the Department is participating will be coordinated through the new Defense Agency.

- Expand public-private partnerships. Finding our missing personnel is a national priority in which many private organizations and individuals are actively engaged. Many of the Department's successes in this area are due to assistance from private citizens and groups. The Department of Defense will take steps to enhance collaboration with private entities in the United States and overseas. The new Defense Agency will be responsible for building and managing these vital relationships with private entities.

The consolidation of the organizations that work on past conflict personnel accounting is a necessary start but we must also change the culture of personnel accounting and processes in place. The Secretary's decision to increase private-public partnerships, make a medical examiner the identification authority and director of laboratory functions, and focus on families as the customer for services are emblematic of the cultural and process changes that must happen for us to be successful in fully accounting for personnel missing from past conflicts.

Some of these decisions, particularly on the role of the medical examiner, are significant departures from how the Department has operated in the past, and will require continued support for change from within the Department and from Congress. The Secretary's decisions are deliberate and backed by years of solid analysis from within the government and by independent bodies. To build on our strengths and to change the cultures, structures, and processes, we must approach this process rationally, not based on emotion or personal agendas and bias. The Department will ensure that we sustain and further develop the strengths of our past conflict personnel accounting processes, notably scientific independence and validity, while increasing the assets available to the mission from the Armed Forces Medical Examiner System.

Immediately following the Secretary's announcement, the Administration developed a legislative proposal that sought specific authorities to help the Department implement the Secretary's direction. I want to thank you, Mr. Chairman and Ms. Davis and all the members of this Committee who worked with the Department to ensure this out-of-cycle legislative proposal was included in the proposed Fiscal Year 2015 National Defense Authorization Act. Without your help, we cannot change the way the Department accounts for its missing service members.

In coordination with the USD (C) and the Director of CAPE, the Department is seeking reprogramming of funds for the three current organizations in FY 2014. The Department will also begin the process of codifying the new Defense Agency in a Department of Defense Directive, and will amend other Instructions and Directives, as required.

Our goal is for the new Defense Agency to achieve Initial Operational Capability by January 1, 2015, and Full Operational Capability by January 1, 2016. Throughout this process, operations to account for the missing and to keep their families informed will continue.

Conclusion

The Secretary of Defense has a longstanding personal interest in this important mission, and feels compelled to improve the Department's operations in support of this critical undertaking. I have welcomed the time I've spent working this noble mission. I have particularly appreciated working with this Committee and others in Congress to help the Department achieve its goal of transforming its past conflict personnel accounting to more effectively account for our missing personnel and to ensure that their families receive timely and accurate information.

Thank you for your continued support and I look forward to your questions.

Michael D. Lumpkin

**Assistant Secretary of Defense,
SO/LIC, Performing Duties,
Under Sec. of Defense for Policy**

Michael D. Lumpkin is currently the Assistant Secretary of Defense for Special Operations/Low-Intensity Conflict (SO/LIC), performing the duties of the Under Secretary of Defense for Policy. When performing the duties of USD (P), Mr. Lumpkin provides advice and assistance to the Secretary of Defense and Deputy Secretary of Defense on all matters concerning the formulation of national security and defense policy and the integration and oversight of DoD policy and plans to achieve national security objectives.

Mr. Lumpkin was sworn in as the Assistant Secretary of Defense for Special Operations/Low-Intensity Conflict (SO/LIC) on December 2, 2013, following his nomination by President Barack Obama and confirmation by the U.S. Senate.

In his role as Assistant Secretary (SO/LIC), Mr. Lumpkin is the principal advisor to the U.S. Secretary of Defense on Special Operations and Low Intensity Conflict. He is responsible primarily for the overall supervision, to include oversight of policy and resources, of special operations and low intensity conflict activities. These activities include: counterterrorism, unconventional warfare, direct action, special reconnaissance, foreign internal defense, civil affairs, information operations, and counter-proliferation of weapons of mass destruction. In his role as Assistant Secretary (SO/LIC), Mr. Lumpkin also oversees the Department of Defense counter-narcotics program, building partnership capacity initiatives and humanitarian and disaster relief efforts.

Prior to his assuming duties as Assistant Secretary (SO/LIC), Mr. Lumpkin served as a Senior Executive at both the Department of Defense and Department of Veterans Affairs. His previous positions include Special Assistant to the Secretary of Defense, Principal Deputy Assistant Secretary of Defense for (SO/LIC), and Deputy Chief of Staff for Operations at the Department of Veterans Affairs. Mr. Lumpkin has also significant experience in the private sector where he served as the Chief Executive Officer (CEO) at Industrial Security Alliance Partners and Executive Director of Business Development at ATI.

Mr. Lumpkin has more than 20 years of active duty military service as a US Navy SEAL where he held every leadership position from platoon commander to Team commanding officer. Mr. Lumpkin has participated in numerous campaigns and contingencies throughout the world to include both Operations Iraqi Freedom and Enduring Freedom.

Mr. Lumpkin holds a MA from Naval Postgraduate School in National Security Affairs. He is a recognized subspecialist in Special Operations/Low-Intensity Conflict and Western Hemisphere Affairs.

DOCUMENTS SUBMITTED FOR THE RECORD

JULY 15, 2014

GLENN "GT" THOMPSON
5TH DISTRICT, PENNSYLVANIA

124 CANNON HOUSE OFFICE BUILDING
WASHINGTON, DC 20615-3805
(202) 225-5121
(202) 225-5796 (FAX)

http://thompson.house.gov

AGRICULTURE
Chairman, Subcommittee on
Conservation, Energy, and Forestry

EDUCATION & THE WORKFORCE

NATURAL RESOURCES

Congress of the United States
House of Representatives

Statement for the record as prepared by
The Honorable Glenn 'GT' Thompson (PA-05)

House Committee on Armed Services, U.S. House of Representatives
Subcommittee on Military Personnel

Hearing on: Review and Restructure of the Prisoner of War/Missing in Action (POW/MIA) Office and Agencies

Tuesday, July 15, 2014

Chairman Wilson, Ranking Member Davis, and Members of the Subcommittee,

Thank you all for the opportunity to submit comments for today's hearing. I appreciate and thank you for your tireless efforts in support of our nation's brave service men and women, including those who served and never made it home.

As the Subcommittee reviews and considers the future of the POW/MIA Office and Agencies, it is essential to ensure that the Department of Defense is correctly prioritizing recovery missions. Recent problems and mistakes raise concerns that deserve our immediate attention, including a troubling situation that has arisen within the Joint POW/MIA Accountability Command (JPAC), which involves the case of Major Lewis P. Smith III, a constituent of mine who was listed as Missing in Action in May of 1968.

Major Smith was trained on the T-38 and C130 aircraft, and was assigned to the 20th Tactical Air Support Squadron, Pleiku Air Base. During combat in Vietnam, Major Smith piloted a Cessna O2A "Sky Master" aircraft in Saravane Province, Laos. During the mission, Smith encountered enemy fire, resulting in the crash of his plane. Electronic signals were heard at the scene, indicating that he had survived the crash, but he was not rescued, and is now honored on the Vietnam Veterans Memorial: Panel 62W - - Line 2.

Major Smith's family has been working with JPAC for many years to recover his remains. The excavation site in Laos is has been on the list for over three years and the

TITUSVILLE
127 WEST SPRING STREET, SUITE C
TITUSVILLE, PA 16354
(814) 827-3985   (814) 827-7307 (FAX)

ERIE COUNTY
(814) 217-9457

PRINTED ON RECYCLED PAPER

BELLEFONTE
3555 BENNER PIKE, SUITE 101
BELLEFONTE, PA 16823
(814) 353-0215 (814) 353-0218 (FAX)

Congressman Glenn 'GT' Thompson
Page 2

trip to excavate the crash site has been postponed twice, allegedly due to budget pressures and sequestration.

Following these events, Major Smith's family reached out to me to help with their efforts to bring Major Smith's remains home. Over the past several months I have worked with the House Appropriations Committee to ensure the accounts for JPAC are fully funded. Despite this work, Major Smith's family recently received devastating news that the recovery site in Laos had been flooded by a newly built dam. As a result, the task of recovering Major Smith's remains has been exponentially complicated.

Furthermore, the dam construction in Laos was planned and built over the course of a decade. During that time, JPAC was fully aware of this project, yet failed to complete the mission before it was too late. This series of events brings into question the adequacy of coordination between JPAC and officials from partner nations and the process by which JPAC prioritizes recovery missions. Ultimately, I remain concerned that JPAC's failure to recover this site could have been prevented. If this is found to be the case, corrective action must be taken to ensure this does not reoccur in the future.

It is vital that families do not have to experience the repeated anguish of losing a loved one for a second time because of an avoidable oversight, such as what happened to Major Smith's family in Pennsylvania. Those who made the ultimate sacrifice for our country and their family members deserve much better.

Thank you again for your help and consideration.

Sincerely,

Glenn 'GT' Thompson
Member of Congress